VIKING
SETTLERS

CONTENTS

Designed and Produced by DAVID SALARIYA
Editor   SHIRLEY WILLIS
Design Assistant   CAROL ATTWOOD

Copyright © The Salariya Book Company 1992

First published in 1992 by
PAN MACMILLAN CHILDREN'S BOOKS
A division of Pan Macmillan Limited
Cavaye Place, London SW10 9PG

ISBN 0-333-55638-0 (Macmillan hardback)
ISBN 0-330-32481-0 (Piccolo paperback)

Reprinted in hardback and paperback 1992

A CIP catalogue record for this book is available from
the British Library
Typesetting by C.S.T. (Hove) Ltd
Printed in Hong Kong

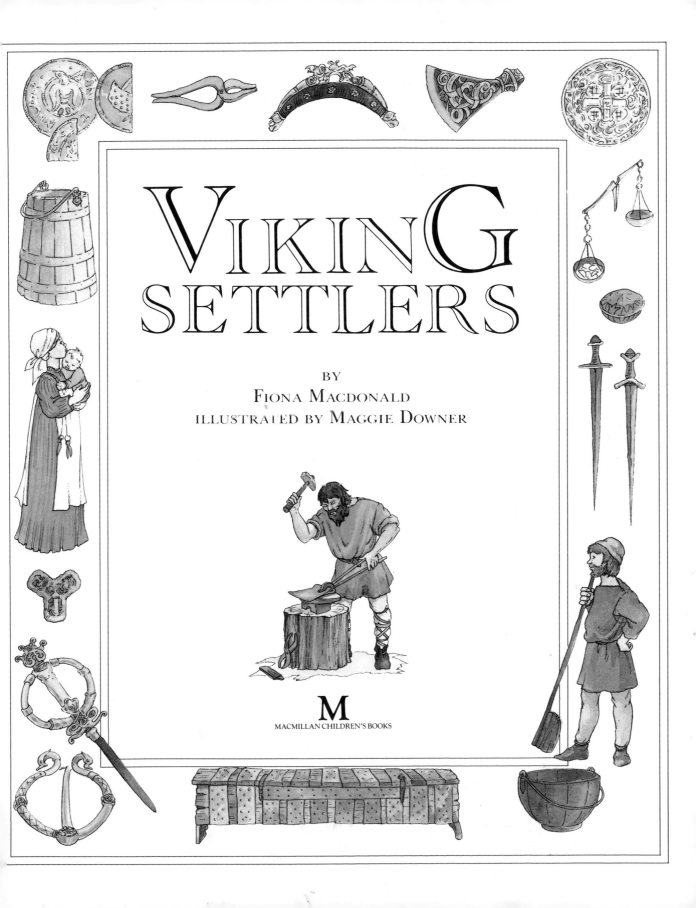

VIKING
SETTLERS

BY
FIONA MACDONALD
ILLUSTRATED BY MAGGIE DOWNER

M
MACMILLAN CHILDREN'S BOOKS

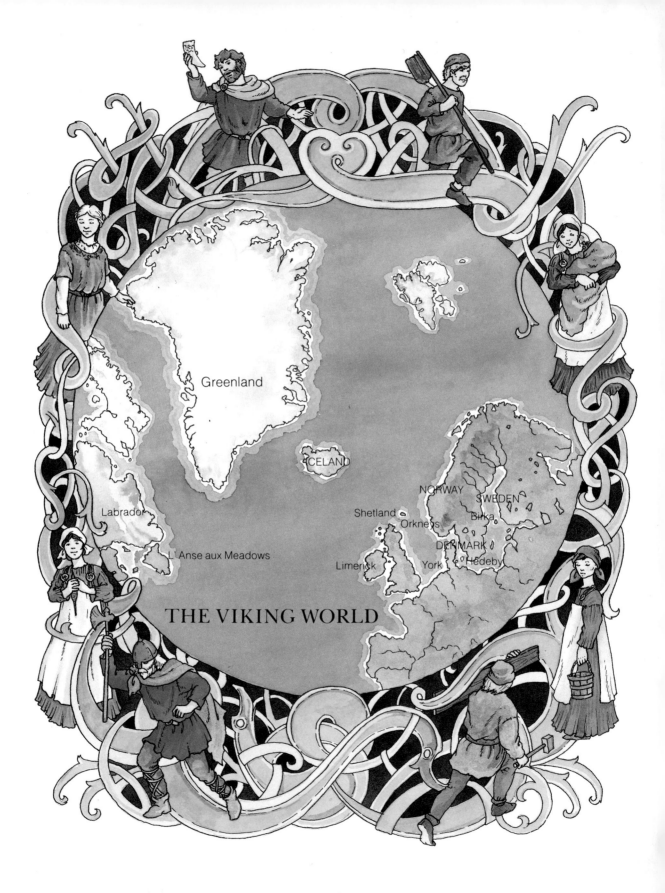

Greenland

ICELAND

NORWAY

SWEDEN

Shetland

Orkneys

Birka

DENMARK

Labrador

Hedeby

L' Anse aux Meadows

Limerick

York

THE VIKING WORLD

INTRODUCTION

The Viking people lived in the north of Europe over a thousand years ago. Their homes were in Norway, Denmark and Sweden, but Viking merchants and warriors travelled to distant lands, trading and fighting. Many Vikings, like the people in this book, came south and settled in Britain, France and Spain. Others journeyed eastwards, to Russia and beyond. A few brave Viking adventurers sailed across the stormy Atlantic ocean, to found a new colony in North America.

The great age of Viking power lasted from about 780–1070 AD. The Vikings and their warships vanished long ago, but traces of the Viking past are all around us. We use many Viking words today, such as "happy", "egg", "sister", "knife" and "ill". We can see the remains of Viking buildings and burial mounds. Viking poems, songs and sagas have survived. Many European museums contain splendid Viking swords, helmets, coins and jewels.

THE VIKING HOMELANDS

Life in the Viking homelands could be harsh. In many places the soil was thin and stony, and everywhere the winters were long and bitterly cold, with months of snow and ice.

The Vikings lived in scattered villages. They built their homes in sheltered bays and inlets by the edge of the sea, because they found the best soil there, as well as streams of fresh water and a safe harbour for their boats. They sailed along the coast to visit (or sometimes to attack) their neighbours; it was easier to travel by water than across the rough, rocky ground.

Viking society was divided into three main groups: lords and warriors, free farmers, and servants.

Families were very important to the Vikings. They provided love, care, protection against enemies and a sense of belonging.

Most Viking homes were farmhouses, where grandparents, parents and children all lived and worked together, under one roof. Powerful warriors, called "jarls", owned several farms, as well as valuable horses, weapons and jewellery. Servants, called "thralls", did all the jobs like gathering wood, cutting peat or spreading manure.

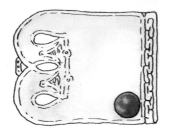

The Vikings loved fine clothes. A heated glass ball and a whalebone board were used to smooth out linen tunics.

FOOD, FISHING AND FARMING

The Vikings were great sailors and fishermen. The fish they caught were eaten fresh or hung outside in the wind to dry so that they would last until winter, when it was too cold to go to sea. Then, men and boys went hunting, trapping birds, rabbits and hares, or shooting deer with bows and arrows.

The Vikings were also farmers, who grew barley, oats and rye. Their wives ground these grains to bake coarse, dark bread, or cooked them with milk to make a thick porridge. For vegetables, they grew peas, beans, turnips and cabbages. Children gathered wild garlic, mushrooms, nuts and berries from the forests. Women concocted medicines from herbs, to take away pain and soothe fevers.

Household tools: dish and ladle, wooden tub, pottery jar, tall wooden bucket, spade, pitchfork and shovel.

Viking farmers kept some livestock: sheep to provide wool, while cows and goats supplied milk, butter and cheese. Chickens, geese and ducks provided eggs, meat and soft, fluffy feathers for quilts.

Travel and Trade

Viking blacksmiths made weapons and farm tools.

Merchants travelled far to Viking market towns.

Not all Vikings were farmers, who made a living from the countryside, or warrior jarls, who became rich through war and plunder. Some Vikings were traders. They bought and sold an astonishing range of goods produced in Viking lands, from beeswax and iron bars to fur coats and walrus tusks. And merchants from overseas – Spain, India and the Middle East – visited the great Viking market towns at Hedeby and Birka, with rare and precious goods to sell.

Viking merchants travelled from Russia in the north to Turkey and Tunisia in the south. They exchanged fish, timber, amber, leather and silver jewellery for wine, silken cloth, glassware, precious stones and coins made of solid gold. Swords and armour made by Viking metal-workers were highly prized.

There was also a slave-trade. Viking merchants sold women and children, captured in raids or bought from Russian slave-dealers, to be shipped off to distant lands.

Above: silver brooches and necklace.

Map: Viking trade routes.

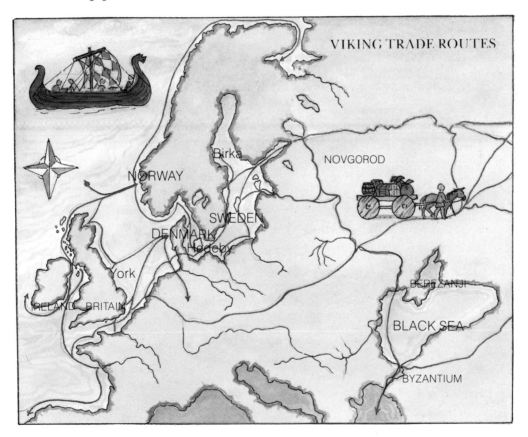

THE WOLVES FROM THE SEA

Viking poems describe the excitement of setting off in search of adventure: travelling across the waves in a fast ship; making a surprise raid on an undefended village; joining in the fight to seize rich plunder; and celebrating over a drunken feast once the fighting was over.

Viking men valued courage, strength and daring more than anything else. Today, we might think of them as bloodthirsty and cruel, but in their own eyes they were heroes, willing to risk death to win fame and rich rewards.

Throughout Europe, kings, lords and ordinary people lived in fear of a Viking attack. They offered the Vikings money and rich gifts to keep away.

The Vikings had always fought among themselves, but from around 780 AD, they began to make raids further south, towards other countries in Europe. In 787 AD they made their first attack on England; in 793 they destroyed the monastery at Lindisfarne. More raids followed, and by 877, they controlled all of eastern England, and most of north-eastern France. They attacked Ireland, Spain, Italy and North Africa as well.

This wooden dial helped Vikings to steer their ships in the right direction. The top hand points to the position of the sun at mid-day.

Vikings treasured their ships. They were given names such as "Wave Walker" or "Long Serpent".

TRAVELLING SOUTH

The first Vikings to arrive in England and France were raiders, but soon other more peaceful visitors began to travel south from the Viking homelands. They came to settle, not to fight. Why did they leave their farms in the north, and how did they make the dangerous crossing to their new homes in a foreign land?

The Viking settlers came south because they were running short of space at home. Viking families had large numbers of children – songs and poems tell us that wealthy men had eight or nine sons (daughters are not mentioned). There was not enough good land to provide each son with a farm. Viking raiders saw that the soils were more fertile and the weather was warmer in the southern lands.

Viking freemen met regularly to discuss village affairs. Each man could speak and vote on future plans for the community.

The Viking settlers travelled by ship. Viking longships were well designed and strongly made. They were built of wooden planks, carefully shaped and fitted together, and beautifully decorated. They were powered by the wind (using a single square sail) or by men rowing with oars.

LEAVING HOME

What did it feel like to leave your Viking homeland and set sail for a new and unknown country? We do not know for certain what the Viking settlers felt as they packed up all their household goods, and stowed them away on board ship. Probably they were sad and scared and hopeful all at once.

But Viking families realised that they faced food shortages and even starvation if they stayed at home. There was the chance of a better life across the sea. And so they packed their boats with everything they could carry. They took their frightened farm animals and all their farm equipment – ploughs, rakes, spades, sacks and harnesses for their horses; tools for building and woodworking, ropes and cloth for repairing sails, cooking pots, looms for weaving, clothes, weapons, jewellery, feather beds and blankets.

Viking sagas tell us that people loved their fields and farms, and were miserable if they left them. They also tell us that Viking sailors knew they might be drowned if their ship was caught in a sudden storm. Experienced travellers frightened their companions with stories about sea-monsters (probably whales), whirlpools and icebergs.

SAILORS AND EXPLORERS

VIKING EXPLORATION

Viking ships were strong, fast and very graceful. They were also surprisingly small. The remains of several Viking longships have survived – a typical ship might measure 25 metres long, 5.5 metres wide, and 2 metres deep. A ship this size carried 50 or 60 people; on a long voyage, they must have felt so cramped. They must also have been wet and cold – the open hull could be covered to protect the cargo, but this provided little shelter for the passengers or crew.

Viking exploration routes across the North Atlantic ocean.

Ship's weather-vane, to show the wind direction.

In 986 AD, Viking explorers set up a colony in Greenland, and, shortly afterwards, began their pioneering voyages westward towards America. Although these journeys are recorded in several Viking sagas, for a long time historians did not believe that the little Viking ships had actually crossed the Atlantic. But in 1961 the remains of a Viking village were discovered on the east coast of Canada. This proved that the saga evidence was true: Viking sailors had reached the New World.

Rune stone, telling a story in pictures.

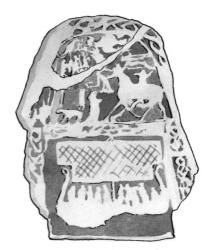

18

Timber framework of a
Viking house in
Iceland.

Vikings had little
furniture – only beds,
tables and stools. This
wooden bed had a
feather-filled mattress.

The bed-posts are
decorated with carved
horses' heads.

A New Home

Once they had safely arrived in their new countries, the Viking settlers had to find somewhere to live. Sometimes they drove the local people from their homes and then moved in themselves. Sometimes they settled on land that had never been inhabited. The earliest settlers probably made rough shelters, like tents, out of their ships' sails and branches from trees. But they soon built strong new houses, very like the ones they had left behind in the Viking homelands.

First, they constructed a framework of thick wooden poles. To make the walls, they wove thin branches and twigs between the poles, then covered them with clay or mud mixed with animal hair. The roof-timbers were covered with a thick layer of straw or reeds, or else with squares of turf. Floors were made of stamped down earth. There was a narrow doorway, with curtains, but no windows, as they would be too draughty. Stables and barns were built in the same way.

FEASTING

If all the settlers worked hard together their new village would soon take shape. Then it would be time to celebrate, with a feast for all the villagers, and songs and music provided by professional poets, known as "skalds". The skald might compose a song in praise of the jarl who had led the settlers across the sea, and who was now the most important man in the new village. He might sing about great Viking victories, and brave deeds in battle. Or he might entertain

At this special feast, Viking women and men are sitting together at table. This was unusual; normally men ate together, and women served them. Women and children then had their meals after the men had eaten.

everyone with well-known stories about heroes, monsters, dwarves, trolls and dragons.

The village women would cook special dishes for the feast. For once, everyone would have plenty of meat to eat, rather than the usual fish, soup and porridge. The villagers would also wear their best clothes and jewellery. Viking women and their servants were skilled at spinning wool, weaving cloth and sewing clothes for all the family. Only the wealthiest people could afford to buy things ready-made from travelling merchants, or in the towns.

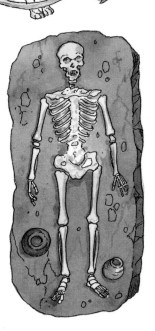

Viking gods and goddesses. Vikings believed that the gods helped them in daily life and protected them in battle.

Ordinary people were buried in simple graves, with their goods beside them.

DEATH AND BURIAL

Viking people were familiar with sickness and death. Men were killed in battle, drowned at sea or injured while working on the farm. Women died in accidents at home or while giving birth. Men, women and children all died from various infectious diseases or, occasionally, from starvation and the bitter cold.

The Vikings believed that people's spirits went on living after their bodies were dead. So they provided their dead friends with everything they might need in the next world: a warrior was buried with his sword and shield, a princess was given jewellery, a comb and a mirror. Archaeologists have found objects like these in many Viking graves.

Great Viking leaders might be burned after they died. The Vikings believed that this helped their spirits to escape from their bodies quickly and easily. Towards the end of the Viking age, many people became Christians and the old funeral customs were forgotten.

24

25

Time Chart

Vikings

c 500 Trade between Vikings and merchants from distant lands expands.

787 First Viking raid on England.

793 Viking attacks on rest of Europe.

862 Viking kingdom established in Russia.

c 800–871 Vikings settle in eastern England.

911 Vikings win control of Normandy (northern France) and settle there.

1066 Normans (Vikings living in Normandy) invade and capture England. William the Conqueror becomes King of England.

1071 Vikings capture southern Italy and Sicily and establish kingdom there.

c 1100 Viking power begins to fade. Vikings living in France, England and Italy have now settled down and mixed with local peoples. New, powerful kings and princes rule in Europe.

Rest of Europe and Middle East

449 Angles, Saxons and Jutes begin to settle in England.

c 450–1000 Peoples of Europe are converted to Christianity.

476 Collapse of Roman Empire in Western Europe. Rise of Byzantine Empire, based in Constantinople (Istanbul).

486 Rise of Frankish kingdom in France and Germany.

c 570–632 The prophet Muhammad preaches religion of Islam.

c 650 Islamic civilisation in Middle East flourishes from now on.

711 Muslims rule in Spain.

800 Charlemagne crowned Holy Roman Emperor, rules over France and Germany.

959 England becomes a united kingdom for the first time.

1096 First Crusade starts – Christian armies invade Holy Land.

Asia and Africa

c 300–700 Buddhist faith spreads through Far East.

320–480 Powerful Gupta Empire flourishes in India.

c 520 Important discoveries in mathematics by Indian scholars.

658 Chinese rule over vast empire in Central Asia and Far East.

c 700–850 Great age of Chinese poetry; Chinese invent paper-making and printing.

c 700–1000 Islamic faith and civilisation spreads throughout Asia, North and East Africa.

c 700 Powerful Ghana Empire rules in West Africa.

c 890 Elegant civilisation flourishes in Japan.

c 1000 Great age of Chinese painting and porcelain.

c 1000 New kingdom founded at Zimbabwe.

c 1080 Chola Empire powerful in India; many beautiful temple-cities built.

North and South Americas

c 300–500 Native American chieftains (known as 'Hopewell Indians') powerful in North America. They build palaces and temples.

c 600–800 Great city-states rule in the Andean region of South America.

c 200–750 Powerful city-states established in Mexico.

c 600 Maya Empire rules over Central and (parts of) South America; Mayas produce great temples and stone-carvings.

c 850 Maya Empire collapses.

c 990 Inca peoples, living in Peru (South America), conquer nearby lands and establish an empire.

c 1000 Vikings sail to Greenland and then on to North America. Vikings build settlement on the east coast of Newfoundland (Canada). Vikings meet Native American peoples and exchange goods.

c 1100 Rise of Toltec Empire, based in Mexico.

Word List

Amber Pretty yellow "stones" used to make Viking jewellery. Although amber looks like shiny pieces of rock, it is really fossil resin, a sticky gum which oozes from tree trunks.

Archaeologists People who study the remains of past civilisations.

Barley A plant which provides grain for people and animals to eat.

Beeswax A sweet-smelling substance produced by bees, used to polish wood and leather.

Burial mounds Heaps of earth, like little hills, used to cover the grave where a Viking chief was buried.

Cargo Goods being carried from one place to another, usually by sea.

Coarse Rough and lumpy.

Colony A new settlement in a distant land.

Concocted Mixed together. Wise Viking women concocted medicines by mixing plants with wine and honey.

Constructed Built.

Fertile Good for growing crops.

Grave The place where someone is buried.

Greenland A large island in the North Atlantic ocean, almost halfway between Europe and America. The climate there is very cold. Some of the land is covered with snow and ice all year round.

Ground Broken into very small pieces. Viking women ground grains of barley, oats and rye between heavy stones to make flour. It was hard, tiring work.

Hull The "body" of a ship; the part that floats in the water, and which carries people and cargo.

Infectious diseases Illnesses that people catch from one another, such as colds, flu, measles and chickenpox.

Inhabited Lived in.

Inlet A strip of sea (like a wide river) stretching inland.

Jarls Wealthy Vikings, who were warriors and war-leaders.

Lindisfarne An island off the north-east coast of England.

Livestock Farm animals, such as horses, cows, sheep and goats.

Loom A wooden framework on which threads are woven together to make cloth.

Monastery The building, usually next to a church, where monks live.

New World North and South America.

Oats A plant which provides grain for people and animals to eat.

Peat A crumbly black substance, rather like soft coal, made from the remains of moss and other plants which grow in marshy areas. The Vikings burned peat to keep warm.

Plunder Valuable goods seized in Viking raids.

Quilts Warm bed-covers, made of feathers sandwiched between two layers of cloth.

Reeds Plants like very thick, strong grass. Reeds were cut and tied in bundles to make warm waterproof roofs for Viking houses.

Rye A plant which provides grain for people and animals to eat.

Sagas Old stories, telling the history of the Viking peoples. Sagas were memorised by Viking men and passed on to their sons. They were finally written down in the Middle Ages.

Skalds Travelling poets and musicians

Thralls People who were not free to choose where to live or work. They could be bought and sold by their masters. They could not take part in discussions about their village. Many thralls were seized in Viking raids. Others were the children of thralls, or had been made thralls as punishment for their crimes.

Turf Thick squares of earth, with grass still growing on it. Turf was used to make roofs on some Viking houses.

Viking homelands The lands where the Vikings first lived: Norway, Denmark and Sweden.

Walrus tusks The long front teeth of walruses. (A walrus is an animal, like a very big seal, that lives in cold, northern seas.) Vikings killed walruses and used their tusks to make jewellery and other precious objects.

Warship A fast ship used for fighting. Viking warships were designed to sail in shallow water, so the Viking raiders could make a quick getaway after their attacks on farms and villages along the coast.

Whirlpool A huge "hole" in the sea, caused by waves and underwater currents. Ships were sometimes sucked into whirlpools, and their passengers were drowned.

INDEX

NOTE: References to illustrations are in bold

Notes for Teachers on History in the National Curriculum

The new National Curriculum for History, which lays down a prescribed course of study for pupils aged five to fourteen plus, was introduced into schools in England and Wales during the autumn term 1991.

This series of books has been designed to provide background information relevant to the designated Core History Study Units for Key Stage 2 (i.e., for pupils aged seven to eleven), and also to the Optional History Study Units at the same Key Stage level. Younger children, in particular, should find the short, simple text and largely visual presentation of information appropriate to their needs.

Viking Settler relates in particular to Core Unit HSU 1 – Invaders and settlers: Romans, Anglo-Saxons and Vikings in Britain. In the words of the National Curriculum Final Programme of Study (HMSO, March 1991, p 19):

"Pupils...should have opportunities to learn how British society was shaped by invading peoples. The focus should be on Roman, Anglo-Saxon and Viking invasions and settlements and on Britain as part of a wider European world...Pupils should have opportunities to study in greater depth ONE of the three invasions, the motives which prompted it, the way of life of settlers...They should be taught about reasons for invasion; way of life of settlers; the legacy of settlement."

All are covered in this book.